DOMINIRICAN LOVE POETRY

By

Angelica Acevedo

ISBN: 1-4140-3862-3 (e-book)
ISBN: 1-4140-3861-5 (Paperback)

Library of Congress Control Number: 2003098848

This book is printed on acid free paper.

Printed in the United States of America
Bloomington, IN

1stBooks - rev. 12/31/03

INTRODUCTION

I was born and raised in Lawrence, MA, and the oldest of three children. My father's name is Rigoberto Acevedo, a Puerto Rican man who is very proud of his culture and children. My mother's name is Fatima Angelina Acevedo, a Dominican woman dedicated to helping others as a clinical nurse assistant at the Greater Lawrence Family Health Center in Lawrence, MA. My brother Luis Acevedo, is interested in following the engineering career and is in the Army National Guard. Finally, my sister Yvonne Acevedo, is a Sociology major who will continue doing well in life and is very interested obtaining her own home.

After Lawrence High School, Class of 1997, I went on to attend a prestigious, private, women's college Mount Holyoke College for the next four years majoring in Psychology with a minor in Spanish. Once I graduated, Class of 2001, I went on to do several jobs in my local area, but I decided that I should advance my degree to enhance my chances in pursuing the social work field. I am currently pursuing my Masters in Social Work at Simmons College in Boston, Massachusetts. I started school in the Fall 2002. I thank you for allowing me to expose a little part of myself and I sincerely hope you enjoy this poetry book. Foremost I thank Mount Holyoke College for the great education it has provided me, my family for all the love and support they have given me and for my muses who have guided me through my thoughts and experiences. Thank you!!

BRIEF DESCRIPTION

Most of these poems describe the love I have felt for my partners and myself. I am 23 years old, Latina lesbian who came out recently to my family in the year 2000. I will never forget the look in my mothers face when I first told her that I loved women. I can't come close to explaining this emotion, but for those who try to change my mind, all I can say is I am who I am. Don't try to change others to fit your thought of them because you can't and you might lose them instead. If you are gay or questioning and don't know if you should come out to your parents, all I can say is that you can't change yourself, be true to yourself, and the rest will follow. If life is not full filling you the way you would like then you should choose to make the necessary steps to change. This life is to be enjoyed. I choose life. I hope you enjoy this collection of poetry that has brought me happiness and sorrow. This is a release of emotions that I want to share with you- my readers. Enjoy!

Angelica Acevedo
Jelly2779@yahoo.com
23 years old

TABLE OF CONTENTS

LOVE POEMS

"True Love"

7/26/00

The world holds many

    Beautiful things and beings,

The wave curls its arc-shaped fluorescent tail

    Onto the shore,

As I dream of my true love,

This woman holds the lock to my

    Undying love,

She is what a true goddess exemplifies,

Such things as beauty, intelligence and grace,

How can I compete with such innocence?

I contemplate a world where I could be without her,

And its' unimaginable to see my life

    Without her love.

A warm flame streaks the air like her sweet voice,

The fragrant smell of her body

    Touches mine,

As our heart-pounding bodies meet again,

Is it me? Or am I dreaming for someone

As beautiful and magical as her kiss,

There are times in which we need not

    Speak,

1

For intense stares into our eyes foretells the

Emotions of sexual heat and ecstasy,

The trees can't see or hear what these

Two women hold in their hearts,

That is the love-, which encompasses their lives

Everyday to just

To just

LOVE.

"Loving my baby"

8/18/00

Dew drops

Sunshine

Stars in the sky

Why do these things

Have to shine?

You might ask me how

And why

With one reply

I don't know why

Just like you in my life

I can't deny

My love for you

Has no time

It permeates my soul

Without control

I live this day

And I think to myself

What an ache

To not have you

By my side

But

There will be a time

In which our minds

Will combine

Together once more

Your presence for sure

I will be your sunshine

I'll shine tonight

And all day long

For you my love

I love to love.

Dewdrops

10/26/00

You mean a part of me that has been explored over and over

Yet I know that what I'm feeling is felt by you

And that our paths will be once more together

We are like two stars in the sky

Far apart yet near to the soul

I can't wait to be with you

To listen, cry, and laugh

For once I leave this nest I've created

I will be with you my love

I'm sad not because your happiness does not fulfill me

But because our skies are not so close

Yet so far

But I love you.

And I'll wait for you.

Universal Love

I evolve from a solar universe,
Two phases a day
I look up into the sky
And observe not only beauty
But life.

We humans are cycling through,
Everyday living and dying
Two phases a day
I am living

A cycle continues to come full circle
As life is born
Dreams are accomplished
Destinies are lived upon

Why can't I be that twig feeling
The nestled breeze?
Why must things come to an end?
It's a cycle.

Forming the trees,
Creating oxygen to breathe,
And what price do we pay as humans
When we destroy such things

The price is the future

Two phases a day

Is what might not be

If we stop caring.

Pink Flowers

10/18/00

Pink flowers in a vaz
Filled with sparkling water
A vision of love with
Total desire
My heart is like an open
Flower allowing itself
To be exposed and to grow

This emotion felt by me
Has taken over
The thoughts once hurt before
But now awakened
This new love has opened
Me and taken me into
A journey of everlasting love
A pink flower has filled me.

Good-Bye

Spring 2000

As I sit and wonder why
I feel this pain in my heart
It hurts to let you go
It hurts to feel that you left
Me alone

I have dreamt you as my wife
As my partner in crime
You are everything to me
Then you had to say good-bye

Do you know how it feels?
Do you realize what you've done?
You've hurt me so bad
Tears will not shed

We have been through everything
There will come a time
Where all I can do
Is say good-bye

Goodbye to yesterday
To what we use to be
All those moments are stuck
In my head

No matter where you are
I will be by your side
You are my shining star

You are the apple of my eye
The one that I have dreamt
I know you're not the one

As I sit and wonder why
I wonder how you've been
And what I say to you
Is a farewell goodbye

Goodbye to yesterday
Goodbye to what we were
Goodbye
Goodbye

"I love you"

20 years old

I wish upon a star in the sky
How much I care for you
There are times in my life
Where all I do is think of you.

Tonight, is the night in which we made
Love
It feels like a dream to be with
Someone like you
Could this be heaven sent or something
Very close to it.

I've never felt this way
Where all I do is think of you
I want so much to be with you
To love, to just caress
If we only had some time to be
So close.

Time passes by slowly, and surely,
We will be together just wait and see
It seems like it will last forever

We will hold each other closely

And kiss once more

I love to feel your lips softly on mine

I love you, you love me

That's the way it ought to be

Together…forever we will be.

My Dear Friend

8/18/99

I reflect the many moments we sat
On your soft, high bed
Words and sentences streamed through
Our lips recalling the past
And forecasting the future.

The candles in your room gave a
Wondrous smell of flattering essence
Which does not cease to escape your beauty
What about that strong, musky odor
Of Garcia Vega cigar.

I remember inhaling
And coughing all that asthmatic- nicotine crap
But we did enjoy our time together
This is what I love about you.

Your sweet smile brings people
To a new understanding of friendship
Philosophical analogies are frequently
Discussed by your wise words.

Times like these make me realize
What the wind does to me
It makes me warm and cool
Like our lasting friendship.

Friends that will share not
What should be said, but what we
Envision in us to be projected
To the world.

Keep your dreams in the present
Instance: that it will become reality
Value what we have and strive
Not for me, but for yourself.

"True Love"

19 years old (8/99)

Falling in love with you
Is something that I hold true
What a magical place to be
Sitting right beside you

The air in the sky caresses
Me tightly
Just like your hands as
You explore me.

I feel like I am in a spell
One in which has no antidote

Do you know what I would do
To just be with you?
I can't stop thinking about
Your warm lips, beautiful touch
Loving words when we are together

I realize now more than ever
How hard it is to be together
But let's take it one day at a time
Trying to keep an open dialogue

For I want to be in your arms
Forever
You are my one, first true love

Wondering if you knew what
I meant when I said to you
I love you.

Please be careful to love me
And when you can't; let go of me
I know what I want is simple

You're like a rose growing inside
I can't stop thinking of you
I love you so much
What should I do?

You have my heart
Which scares me
Love me unconditionally
For I love you so…

For I have fallen deeply in love with
You
I love you. I love you
Like no one else.

Untitled

10/00

Love

Pain

Laughter

Happiness

Crying

Joy

Amor

Dolor

Felicidad

Llorar

Alegria

All describe what you have meant

To me mother

I saw you light up the sky as

You cooked our dinner

And smiled when we did good

In school

Mami, we tried to make

You proud

You had such a way of looking

At things such innocence

Yet you realized it was

Time to go

I want you to know

My love for you is still shining

Inside of me everyday

I love you mami

See you soon.

Revelation

10/23/00

Existence in this world

Has made me who I am

Friends, family, society, intimate

Lovers, all had made

And shaped me to this

Suffering will not cease

Pain will occur over and over

In a way it's a lesson of life

To take things not for granted

But as a blessing

We might not know what

Tomorrow will hold for us

But we can live this day as

A blessing

Interacting with others

Sharing ideas, spending

Time with close friends

All have a common goal

To form a self-identity

Unique

Not a self-centered, selfish

Person who wants everything

Hey, we are mortal

We are beings connected by

Many things a world that

Gives us air to breathe

A mind to think

Time to acknowledge

Today is not a chance to

Refrain from dreams

But to live them out

To experience all the errors and

Mistakes that we can only learn

From

To be who you are is special

Unique

Beautiful

Take the time to be one with nature

With our world of beings, things, animals

Be who you are but also grow

From those around you

Learn to change

Learn to adapt, Learn to change

"To Love"

12/1/00

That February evening when you

Accompanied me to this gay bar

I thought wow…she wants to

Come okay I hope we have fun

Then we observed the drag show

Laughing and having a good ole time

We danced several songs together

After that night something clicked

I saw you the next night at Wave

You were drinking and looking so beautiful

I always found you attractive, but

Nothing really beyond that point

You see I enjoyed our cool friendship

You had this carefree attitude about

Things, something I need to work on

But there you were this beautiful

Woman in the bathroom

I took my chances and asked you for a tap kiss

Brief…yet it showed me that you cared

This next night we shared in my house

Was magical, revelating, and beautiful

I felt your warm body touching mine

Your sweet kisses upon my lips

And loving hugs as you

Explored parts of me…you

Seemed afraid, but allowed

Yourself the experience in being with a woman

And there this newfound relationship

Sparked. We grew more and more closer

And then you said yes

You became my girl…my love

Ever since that day I have become

The happiest girl.

I'm deeply in love with you

I can't wait to finally be yours

To be with you everyday when you

Wake up in the morning

I'm yours to keep. To be. To love.

"I love you (forever)"

2/14/01

my heart yearns for your touch

your sweet kisses make me want

you more and more and then

there will be a day where

the roses between our legs

will reunite

in one hot day

in that one instant moment

the love we hold deep in our hearts

will exclaim total desire

and emotional tranquility that only

heaven knows

what these two women want

is just that

each other.

"You are like a flower in bloom"

11/12/00

See you have these qualities

this magical spell that has

made me want you more and more

you have this essence

this fragrant smell upon your body

that makes me want you

you have this passion

that evokes such sexual heat

and ecstasy

you have this smile

that lights up the day and makes

me want to be next to you

you have this laughter

its very contagious it makes

me want to be close to you

you have this flower

between your legs that

makes me squirm with desire

you have this beauty

that makes the world go round

and round

you are what I call a flower in bloom

ready to spread its petals

stretching out each day

and allowing itself to breathe

in and out the fresh air

as I come next to this petal

I realize I am

with you.

"Love is a flutter of emotions"

6/6/00

Love is a flutter of emotions in which my heart feels one that has no boundaries or limitations…it just wants to feel the happiness of that special someone…and that is you—my love.

"Eres una rosa"

11/1/00

Mi amor es como una rosa

creciendo en mi corazon

fuertemente

y no puedo pensar

no puedo comer

no puedo banar

me haz lumbrado en mi cosas

bonitas y especiales

quiero encontrar el sentido en cual

me siento quieta

se que me vas a esperar

y yo a ti

y cuando reunimos

voy a recordar el momento

que estoy explicando.

"Chaotic cosmos"

12/15/00

Who am I
I am Puerto Rican and Dominican
born in the United States
citizen of many oppressed people
I count the stars
and see all but suffering
You are the essence of love
I am who I want to be
made by those who love thee

I give my soul all that it can take
because we are solitude
sole survivors of life
my love for you
Breaks all rules
For who you are makes me
Move in directions
never felt before
Images pop in my head
of past moments
We shared together
To be with you is yet

but how can I when
all I do is think of you
I want so much to hold
you inside of me
keep you away from harm
and just be with you
can I just be
and dream of this reality
that fills me

I love you like
an angel sent by god
soul beauty you possess
that evokes me
to be
I need you
I yearn for your touch
your holy essence makes me
quiver with excitement
I feel you
I need you
Keep me.

another miracle

If being in love

hurts as bad as fire

than burn me up

for I want to feel

to be; to think and

dream of you

You see I don't hold

back

I can't because you

give me inspiration

to be who I am

to love the only way I can

that is by being with you

Now

I wish to find a forever

type of love

unconditional like my mother

Mother myself is what I should do

"Torment of a Heart"
1/10/01

Pain Anger Hurt

fills my body as I

deal with this moment

in time…am I what?

No, I'm not. Why must

you say hateful things

that hurt my inner core

I am sad and angry because

all I'm doing is loving you

I asked you once to not

say those words…and all

you did was repeat and repeat

over and over

Why can't you understand?

What this does to me…all I

can do is take a smoke

to calm me down

It means nothing, I know

You were just kidding

Why do you get like this?

I know that is what you will say

I do, because it hurts me

All I wanted to do was just

talk to hear your voice

I called you twice just

because I thought you

didn't hear the phone

But, come to find out

you knew I called before

I will just relax and hope

to calm down

I just wish that you will

become more sensitive to my

feelings as I to yours.

Beautiful Creation

8/21/01

I must say your beauty
Has me mesmerized
It's like a spell
That makes me confused
Yet certain
That you are a beautiful
Black woman.

Your lips are full
Ready to be kissed
Your body is the bombs
Sculpted by almighty God
Your eyes are formed
To cast stares onto
Those who look at you.

You are a beautiful
Black woman
Who has me looking
Crazy—for you
I'll say that
You are beautiful.

"Talk to me"

8/27/01

I talk to you

Because you're the one

I talk to you

Because I love

I love you

I love your smile

I talk to you

I talk to you.

If you only knew

The way I feel for you

If you only knew

That you're the one

You are my baby

You are my life

I talk to you

I talk to you

Because you're the one

I talk to you

Because I love

I love you

I love you

I talk to you

I talk to you.

H20

2/8/01

Raindrops fall onto the earth

It's like a sign for what

We have in store

You see water symbolizes

freedom

wavy cosmetic universes

coming together

forming these water droplets

as it surrounds its location

I see you

As it hits its' target

I breathe you

Moments like these form a

Picture of you and I

Contemplating our lives

Making decisions then what

We have each other

To rely on

To keep us focused and not

So scared

I breathe your energy to commence

A new reflection

A new vision

You and I are like these raindrops

Falling onto each other

Freedom to be

To be my water droplet.

Love, Individual, Community

5/01

Love is what I call a

Wondrous feeling that

Fills the body and soul

Circulating our veins

Our thoughts as we

Turn to the side to

Realize what one

Has in life.

Its' one that can't

Ever be explained in words

It takes over you

Over you

WOW! What a beautiful

Feeling of the mind and heart

Not only does it fill your

Soul, but you are allowed

To share this love with

People like you and I

We and us

This community of these

People form a union

But it can easily break

If ties are not

Spoken too, if not

Acknowledged.

A bond must be

Tight enough to see

This love go beyond

Its limits

It is one that I wish

To have now and

Forever.

I miss you

4/14/01

Don't you know how I feel
I mean don't you realize
What I've gone through
In my life
As I see you…things just disappear
We are like two floating ducks
Going on our merry way
Connecting to each other
Ways in which I have not experienced
before
I miss you like no other
I cry because I want you to be close
To me
I miss your laughter
I miss your smile
I miss our funny conversations as we
End with a kiss
I miss your touch
I miss your presence
You are a strong black woman
One in which I admire totally
For you bring out the best in me
I know time is near
But I can't help how I'm feeling
Because I miss you.

Lonely Nights

5/23/01

Lonely nights in my bed

As I go to sleep

And think of you

And wonder how you've been

I wonder many things

Life is of course a mystery

Yet I'm sure

My love for you runs through

All obstacles and tribulations

I question what I'll do

Once I graduate

The options are there

Yet I'm not sure

I know I have a calling

In life; to make others happy

And not so blue

To make myself happy and

Free from stress

Yet I'm not sure

I love you more than words

Said out loud or even actions

This runs deep that

The stars understand me

That life is great especially

When you meet that person

That makes you tingle inside

That makes you cry without knowing why

That makes you want to be close too

And not so far

And I have you

You are a beautiful woman

A woman who has lots of love

All you have to do is share

And you shall receive

All I want for now

Is to be close to this star

To this sky

To be close to you

Don't be afraid to

Love so deep.

Angelica Acevedo

Butterflies

5/23/01

Butterflies flutter

They play music

To my ears

You see they fly

Across the sky

Fluttering their magic

Wings with delight

For another new day

A new beginning

A time for change

To start something new

And this journey has

Almost begun for me

I am close to reaching

My goal in life

And once that's done

Its time to start

Something new

Someone like you.

My hair

5/23/01

Curly locks

Brown hair

Big ass frizz

As I wake up in

The morning

I wash these brown

Locks and

Wonder how did my

Hair get this curly?

RIP

5/23/01

Brown soft skin

Caressing my body

Her sweet smell and

Cocoa butter has

Me captured.

She has me without

Even knowing

Her gorgeous locks

Twist and twist me

With ecstasy

Building in me

More and more pressure

To unfold my desires

Her brown eyes

Stare at me

And makes me feel like

The world has stopped

It's just her and me

Loving and growing

Being there in that

Instant that we

Can share—she's

My star—my angel

This beautiful black

Woman has

Captured me.

Destiny

5/30/01

Forever might seem like an eternity

But really it has no time limit

It persist within us each day

We breathe, we live, we eat

I like to think of myself

As a star in the sky; shining

Bright and letting others know

There is this present moment

We can share with others that

Shouldn't be taken for granted

I hope to live this day

With all of my heart and soul

I am willing to do so everyday

Give me the strength

Shango to continue on my journey

To everlasting happiness

To be filled by a love

So deep in my heart

I want to feel this love

Everyday of my life.

Who am I

7/9/01

Who am I…

Such a difficult

Question to even

ponder

I am soul

I am funny

And beautiful

Light skinned American girl

With Latino heritage

Running through my veins

Brown eyes, loving to

Stare into the eyes

Of my lover

Lucious lips—wavy brown hair

Upto my shoulders

Who can't miss me.

I'm unique. One of a kind.

Manufactured by God-almighty

Really I'm genuine

At times too blunt

Poetic—brave

And scared

I smoke and like to drink

I have a lot to be thankful for—

My health

My talents

My life

I am ANGELICA—   one of a kind.

Tanto Dolor

9/6/01

No puedo pensar en ti

No puedo pensar en ti

Fuiste mi amor

Y ahora no puedo mas

Mi alma llora por ti

Mi alma llora por ti

Solamente quiero

Dejar este amor

Y continuar mi vida

Sin pensar en ti

No puedo pensar en ti

No puedo pensar en ti

Tengo que olvidar

Y ir con mi vida

Ahora te digo a ti

Que no puedo mas

NO puedo hablar

No puedo mas.

Dejame tranquila

Dejame ahora

No quiero hablar

Siempre te amare

Siempre voy a recordar

Las memorias

Las experiencias

Pero no puedo mas

No puedo mas.

Heart Broken

6/15/01

Worlds apart

My heart

Worlds apart

I feel sharp

Punctures piercing

Through every inch

Of my body

I feel sadness

Cries once in awhile

Sadness, tears

Fill my soul

Each day.

Each day

I am without

You has me

Crazy.

Not crazy for

The total distance

But from the

Distance you

Have created by your
Heart.

You already know the
Answer between us
We both know the
Outcome of yesterday
And last year.

Wow! Has it come
To this—I never
Thought it could
Happen we were
So happy
Yet you said
This might not
Last forever.

You said I
Ask to many
Questions
You broke my heart
You have my heart

What will I do
Without you by

My side
I feel hollow,
Empty, alone
Don't leave me
To this state.

I need you.
I need you.

Can't this workout?
Can't this be like
Old times.
Having a good time
Chatting about our
Love, DR and how
We care for each other.

Damn, girl
What made you
Change your mind
Or who?
For this love I
Hold for you
Is mad, true.

Don't be a sucker
Love me for who
I am and let me
Be your baby.

Why

9/21/01

I don't know why
You said good bye
I don't know why
You had to leave.

I don't know why
You made me cry
I don't know why
You didn't try

This is why I don't
Know why.

I don't know why
You said good bye.

Word by Word

8/7/02

This is a program that

Needs to be explained

It is one that should

Bring a smile upon your face

Children reading to other children

Embracing words and sentences

Dialoguing amongst each other

Expanding their minds

To other worlds

To other imaginary places

This is what we've done

And I hope it

Shall continue on

And on and on

Until the next generation.

United We Stand

8/7/02

Arms to reach

Mouths to talk

Bodies to embrace

And others to watch

We are humans

United with a cause

A human need to be

Understood and loved

We are what we want

To become

We can form a society

To become accepting

Of all races and creeds

We can be just that

UNITED.

Can you feel me?

5/1/02

Can you feel me?

Can you feel me?

When I speak to thee

Do you realize what

I'm saying because

It feels like an open

Hole gaping threw

Plasmic craters formed

In my gaping heart muscles

Contracting every which way

This expression means

That you do not realize

That what your doing

Is hurting me

I know I need to

Move on

You said shit, doesn't last

Forever

But why? Cause I do

I will last forever

In your heart, body and mind

I'm the bombs

I'm the shit

Damn, you had to

Fuck it up

You fucking bitch

Damn, son you

Really did me wrong

Now, what

How do I move on

See other people

Yeah fucking right

I can't even think

Straight

Do you feel me?

Do you?

Cause if you do

Raise your hand

Raise it high

For I don't want

To be alone

Alone in this

Fucking state of mind

That has me

Looking crazy

Looking like a fool

Can I find someone

Who will love me

For me

Who fucking knows

Nah, mean.

Untitled

2/18/02

You are contagious girlfriend
You have a sexy persona
One that makes men and women
Melt-without even knowing why

It's called a gift
To be in your presence
I have moments
That I recall
As a spell
Capturing me into
A feeling of hypnosis

I can't help but love you
For you make me melt
Girlfriend- you are a gift
Don't you forget it

When I leave you again
Don't forget that
You are contagious
And your love has
Me wanting you
More and more.

Tough Woman

4/6/02

Some say that love is a form
Of happiness that caresses
Your every being
And than there are others
Who shout out that
Sadness, pain fills their soul
And will never want to
Feel like that ever again.

I say that if I find the
One- who will shower me
With love, affection and
Unconditional understanding

Than this love will last
And I haven't found her
But, once I do
I will tell you
And that will be the
Beginning of my life.

Memories

6/17/02

My heart flutters with

A distinct rhythm of

Beats that fill my inner core

You see this woman who

Has these qualities like

Passion, a loving smile

And a drive has

Made me melt like no other

She is a woman who I can

Spend countless hours just

Trying to understand her

And then there she is as

Naked as can be in my presence

Allowing me to explore her soul

And there I am loving her

Beauty, her thoughts and her being

Yes, her being is as rapturing

As nothing I can ever understand

I wonder at times how I

Came to have these feelings

Of loving her—but I

Love her so very much

That I can't imagine my

Life without her not even

For one second

This woman is my sky

My star

A part of me

I love you ma

I see our paths in

The very distant future

Come together to

Form a wonderful

Union of souls

That want to live

Life and become

Become

Will become just

That each other.

Love you until our

Skies are close

Not so far

Until I'm with you

Enjoy all life has

To offer.

Te quiero con todo mi

Alma y corazon.

Attitude

7/28/02

You speak to me at a

Certain setting of life

You speak to me and

Tell me I have attitude

I guess that

You don't understand me

I don't have attitude

I am just me

Your not perfect nor I

But this doesn't mean

I can't get mad

Or sad

So, don't say to me

That I have attitude

Cause if I do

Your not far from behind.

Angelica Acevedo

Time to say good-bye

7/28/02

girl you have me all

fucking confused

and out of wack

I don't know from my left

Or right

But its all good

You tell me we are just friends

Good for you

I have been trying for

The past year and a half

To get you back

But then this sign

From up above

Came to my inner thoughts

And said to me

Its time to say good-bye

I say to you

You were my love

My life

And then I realized

Its time for me

And this unhappiness

And this sadness

Can't be filled by

You

So, its time to say

Good-bye

And know that I

Once loved you and

Wish you all the best.

I think I want you back...

9/5/02

What is it to lie in your bed

And feel the presence of

Your lips, thighs and breasts

What is it to sleep by your side

In your glow

And loving smile

You make me laugh with your corny jokes

Your being makes me want

To cry

To be

Just that by your side

Don't leave me here alone

In this dormitory setting

To fixate on books and articles

Just so I can be that

Lonely person I dread not to become

I want us to be in your bed

And dream about our futures

Together

With children and a loving home

Let us dream and become

That reality.

Me

10/6/02

I am Puerto Rican and Dominican

Born in Lawtown

For those who don't know, Lawrence Mass.

I grew up in the ghetto

Poverty was my state of mind

There were times that we had no

Heat or light

But we made it

My parents gave my siblings and me

Plenty of love

We had traditional values

We went to church, we had a two parent

Household, but many problems

Boys and girls were treated differently

My brother went out

We had to stay to clean and cook

The language that was spoken

That was spoken was Spanglish

I learned about my culture, my history

In college

The language of my people

My people were learned in college

I picked up books

I spoke to those who could understand

Where I was coming from

My unrest, my distress, my life

I grew up thinking I was right

I had all the answers

I didn't

I embraced my culture after many years

Of not knowing what my people

Had gone through

I am not only dominirican

But American for I grew up in the USA

What does that mean?

I grew up in a fast society

Money money money

Rang like a clear bell

In my being, my soul

I did not only embrace

My culture

My people

But my sexuality

I am a proud dominirican lesbian

My family loves me for me

This has its own struggles

Of identification that I learned

To embrace

Will god love me for me?

I would think so

I grew up thinking that this

Was a sin

I was going to hell

I don't know

But, I do know that I love

That I care

That I love

And, how can that be wrong!

So, my life is unique

A trying time of struggles

But I know my people

Deserve to be heard

I am telling you my

Story to bring you

Closer to my world

For I love life

I love JELLY.

If loving hurts

2/18/03

how can one love again

when loving hurts

as bad

as fire upon my fingers

sharp, stinging sensations

fill my inner core

If all I have left is me

My intact self

To rely on

And move on from past hurts

I wish I can love

So deep again

I know it will take time

Its just a matter

Of letting go

Of being free with emotions

And realizing there is a risk

A risk worth taking

If given the proper circumstances

Right

Right

I see a new love

As an awakening

Experience from a

Deep, sleep state

That can make me aware

Of my self

Of my being

A lover

A fighter

A romantic

Once again

It's just a matter of time

My love

That I will see this

Light that evokes

Me

That strengthens me

And then

I will love again

It's not you

But me

I need time to

Readjust

To relearn

To let go

To cry

And be with me

To be alone

To be in a state of solitude

Within my core

Within my soul

I will see the light

You'll see.

Languages

2/18/03

Speak to me in Creole

And I shall respond

To you in Spanish

Damn, these images of

Words—floating

To the surface and

Beneath it

Lies you

Lies me

Dreaming of our cultures

As they try to interchange

And communicate

Sac pace

What's up

Bien

Good

So, what does this say

Our exchange

Our dialogue

Can cross borders

Waves-distances

Don't let it get

73

Stuck

Because I will be there

To hold you

And keep you from drowning.

If you only knew...

5/2/03

your love is intoxicating

making me feel all types

of sensations

I can't ever imagine my life

Without your presence

If you only knew

That I hold onto your words

Like they were my own

Its powerful

To be in this state of bliss

Scary at times

Yet invigorating

Your love has filled me

My soul, my being

Has become a part of you

And if I were to let go

I would begin to suffocate

Because your love has

Exposed me

To a part of me

I didn't even know

Was there

My love—my sweet Nubian queen

You are my baby

My soul

My love

Take me into this journey

And open this book

To a new chapter

I'll be there

With open arms.

Untitled

5/21/03

you forgot something
yeah you
you heard me
you forgot something

it's as simple as a
fucking phone call
to let me know
what's up

is it that difficult
for you to do
because if it is
just fucking let me know

I'll be happy to
Discuss this
No, I'm not possessive
I'm not insane
I'm not suffering from OCD

I'm just a woman
Whose in love
Just call
And I'll listen
Just call.

Sadness

9/15/03

Tears run down my face

As memories come back

To hunt me

To hunt my existence

I learned to bury them

To move on, not reflect

To carry on the day

As if nothing has happened

But, I'm hurting

I'm crying inside

As the soul begins to

Cry out

And yell

Please stop

I want to forget

It's not the time

I hold on

And listen to my heart

Telling me

Its okay

To cry

To cry

To cry

Release and you shall

Be free

Be free.

ABOUT THE AUTHOR

I was born and raised in Lawrence, MA, and the oldest of three children. My father's name is Rigoberto Acevedo, a Puerto Rican man who is very proud of his culture and children. My mother's name is Fatima Angelina Acevedo, a Dominican woman dedicated to helping others as a clinical nurse assistant at the Greater Lawrence Family Health Center in Lawrence, MA. My brother Luis Acevedo, is interested in following the engineering career and is in the Army National Guard. Finally, my sister Yvonne Acevedo, is a Sociology major who will continue doing well in life and is very interested obtaining her own home.

After Lawrence High School, Class of 1997, I went on to attend a prestigious, private, women's college Mount Holyoke College for the next four years majoring in Psychology with a minor in Spanish. Once I graduated, Class of 2001, I went on to do several jobs in my local area, but I decided that I should advance my degree to enhance my chances in pursuing the social work field. I am currently pursuing my Masters in Social Work at Simmons College in Boston, Massachusetts. I started school in the Fall 2002. I thank you for allowing me to expose a little part of myself and I sincerely hope you enjoy this poetry book. Foremost I thank Mount Holyoke College for the great education it has provided me, my family for all the love and support they have given me and for my muses who have guided me through my thoughts and experiences. Thank you!!

www.ingramcontent.com/pod-product-compliance
Lightning Source LLC
Chambersburg PA
CBHW020336290526
45785CB00005B/2037